*Releasing the **WEIGHT** of My Past*

Releasing the WEIGHT of My Past

Cynthia H. Robinson

Published by Seaborough Enterprises Publishing, LLC

Savannah, GA

© 2016 Cynthia Robinson

Photography by Magnolia Shade Photography

Seaborough Enterprises Publishing's printed edition

ISBN: 978-0-9841235-3-7

Table of Contents

Acknowledgments

I would like to dedicate this book to my loving husband, Steve Robinson, who has been by my side through thick and thin. He has supported me throughout the years and helped me to become all that God has called me to be. I love you, Babe!

To my mother, who gave me an opportunity for life, and I'm thankful to God for rebuilding our relationship for his glory. To my beautiful children, Tanisha, Dominique, TaShawn, Terrence and Jasmine, who never stopped believing in me. To my grandchildren, Amaya, Kaylah, DeLambra, Dallas and Kingston, who love me unconditionally. To my brother, Frederick Hill with NEXcel Technologies, who built the website for this book and to my one and only sister, Tracey Whitaker; love you, Tracey.

To my Pastors, Vince and Marcia Allen, who taught me to step out on faith and not to be afraid to do the things that God has placed in me. Pastor Marcia poured so much love into my life in the beginning of my walk with The Lord, and Pastor Vince has always pushed me to go outside of my comfort zone.

To my friends who inspired me to walk in the purpose that God has designed for me. Bridget Alcide, who is a great friend and helped with the editing of this book, and who also encouraged me when I felt like I couldn't do it; Geneva Turner, an amazing woman of God that is not afraid to share her wisdom; Janice Mitchell with Brave Marketing, for her friendship and marketing skills; Renita Tiller, my prayer partner, who helped me pray through the birthing of this book; Cathy

Graves, who was very supportive in the beginning stages and helped me to be transparent enough to talk about my past to her; Latrilla Nolan, who is a helpful undercover prayer warrior; Brittney Baxter, who did my beautiful photo shoots; and a host of other friends and family that I know are praying for my success.

Foreword
By Pastor Vince Allen

Cynthia's story is the epitome of Genesis 2:25, when God said of Adam and his wife; "They were both naked and were not ashamed."

This type of transparency is rare, even when it seems in today's society that people "tell-all" on social media and reality TV. The faith and fortitude exemplified by Cynthia speak of her spiritual growth and BIGness of God on the inside of her.

From my first encounter with her in 1997, I realized Cynthia had many insecurities and hidden hurts. Nevertheless, today she stands as an overcomer, a victor, and a champion, having defeated the "Goliaths of her past."

The words in this book have healing power! There is no doubt in my mind that multitudes of people, both women and men, young and old, will experience the liberating power of Jesus Christ and the Cross because of Cynthia's obedience.

This is a proud moment for me, and I am so proud of you!

With love,

Pastor Vince

Introduction
Releasing the WEIGHT of My Past

By Cynthia H. Robinson

I must say, in all of my 51 years of living on this earth, writing this book is the hardest thing that I have ever done! Writing my life down on paper is a new experience for me. It's like looking into a window of someone else's life, or being a fly on the wall in a stranger's room. I cried, even mourned for the little girl in this story. I had to relive difficult moments and feelings that I have spent most of my life trying to bury.

I had to tap into those feelings that I didn't want to feel anymore. I had to reach into that dark place I preferred not to go to, but I know that this is the timing of Almighty God to tell this story.

As I begin to write this book, so many questions are going through my mind:

- Who will want to read it, since I'm not a famous author?

- How will my friends and family look at me going forward, knowing everything that I went through?

- Will this book cause someone to be set free from their past pains?

- Or will this be just another book that sits on the shelf and collects dust?

I am just being real! I think of myself as a pretty straightforward person, so I don't want to hold back on the things I believe God is allowing me to release in this time and season. My prayer is:

- That you will be encouraged and inspired to move forward in life without self- imposed limitations.

- That this book will help women who have experienced abuse in their past to break free of any strongholds.

- That this will help mothers with young children to be more aware of who they allow to take care of their children.

- That you will enjoy the journey of life to the fullest.

- That you will take the limits off of your mindset, release your past to Jesus, and know that nothing is too hard for Him!

I am thankful for my life in Christ, because I don't know where I would have ended up if I had not met him. As I reflect on some books that I have read that really had a great impact and made a difference in my life, my prayer today is that the person who reads this book will walk away changed, totally set free from the pain of their past, encouraged to move forward and, most of all, that they will desire a relationship with my Lord and Savior Jesus Christ.

"The Child Within"

Part I

It all began one spring day, when a school bus driver parked on our street and began talking to my mom and the other ladies that lived in the apartment complex near 23rd Street. He drove for the school bus system and for the recreation center. He was very charming and funny to the ladies; he knew how to engage them in different conversations. He performed magic tricks for the children that were playing outside. He came by on the weekends and did tricks, like removing his thumb finger or making money appear and disappear behind our ears. This was very exciting for us kids! He brought us candy and sometimes he gave us the money that he used in the magic tricks. My mom knew his wife from the Parks and Recreation Center, where we spent a lot of our time. I think that's why she felt comfortable having conversations with him; I believe she truly thought he was a nice guy, like we all did.

I don't remember how it happened, but when I was around five years old, the bus driver and his wife became my godparents. I'm not sure why, out of all those children in the neighborhood, they chose me. They came by on the weekends to pick me up, while my other siblings went to my grandparents' house. His wife appeared to be a nice lady in front of my mom, and she acted as if she really cared about me, but behind-the-scenes she was a different person. She was really mean to me; she would pick at me and call me ugly, just like a little child. I wondered why she would take me home with her if she didn't like me. It was really weird; she reminded me of the witch in Hansel and Gretel (how she led the children away with candy and treats, but had an evil motive behind her kindness). I think this is one of the reasons why it was hard for me to trust people. Looking back, for some reason I can't shake this feeling that maybe she knew some of the things that her husband was doing. I also wonder how many other children were led into this trap.

My godparents lived near Wynton Road. My godmother's mother lived with them. She was blind, but so very nice to me. I remember she was overweight and usually sat in a rocking chair for most of the day. She needed assistance to go to bed and to the bathroom. As I look back, I believe she was a Christian because of the glow she had on her. When I was there, she sat in her rocking chair and listened to gospel music on the radio. I felt comfortable with her and loved being around her and her oldest son, Gilbert. I called Gilbert 'uncle'; he didn't live there, but he came and visited his mother all the time. Gilbert and Big Momma were genuinely nice people. Uncle Gilbert couldn't read, so I read to him. That always made my day and I know that it made his day also. He never tried to take advantage of me in any way; he treated me like the child that I was and he was always very kind.

I thought my godfather was the same, until one night I saw a different side of him; a side of him that I had never seen before and didn't like very much.

Part II

I stayed in the guest room at my godparents' house. One night when I got out of bed to go to the bathroom, I felt this person's body come from behind and grab me; he put his hand over my mouth and held me close to him. I was very scared! My breathing was heavy and my heart was beating so fast it felt like it was coming out of my chest. I had no idea why someone would be grabbing me. The hand was very big and smelled like cigarettes.

The person took me into the den, which was close to the bathroom, and told me if I was quiet they would take their hand from my mouth. I became very quiet, so that he would stop squeezing my mouth. When I looked around, I saw it was my godfather; he was staring at me with a crazy look. The room was dark and the only light in the room was coming from the TV and a small lamp sitting on the end table. I noticed on the end table were magazines, napkins, a pack of cigarettes and a lighter. Later on in life I found out that those were called Playboy Magazines. Women were sitting in swimsuits, with their legs wide open and their private area showing. I had no idea what that was so I asked, "What is that?" He proceeded to tell me that I had the same thing that they had (later on that weekend when I was in the bathroom, I remember looking down at my private parts to see if it looked like what I saw; it didn't, because they had a lot of hair and I thought that was gross). He had a video playing with things I had never seen before. I covered my eyes and told him that it was nasty!

I had no idea what time it was, I just knew it was night and everyone else was asleep, so he made sure I was very quiet. He put his hands down my pants and made me sit in his lap. I was shaking because I was so afraid. He kept comforting me and saying, "It's going to be okay." I remember asking, "What are they doing on TV?" He told me that's what men and women did when they loved each other. Then he said, "You know that I love you?" And I said, "Yes, daddy, I love you too." Then he kissed me on my lips. I remember wiping so hard because his slob was on my mouth and he smelled like cigarettes; I didn't like that at all! He asked me with his hands down my pants, "Does that feel good?" I began whining and asked if I could please go back to bed. I kept on whining, and I guess my whining was getting too loud; it seemed to make him uncomfortable, so he let me go. I ran back to the room, buried my head under the covers and cried myself to sleep, saying, "I want to go home; I want to go home." It felt like morning would never come.

Part III

I woke up the next day and packed up my stuff. It was funny because I didn't know how to pack; I just stuffed all my things in my suitcase, and I was ready to go home. I told him that I wanted to go home, but he was extremely nice and bought me ice cream, candy, coloring books and crayons. He told me not to say anything about what happened the night before. I remember just being happy because I had all those treats and so I stayed that night again, but did not get out of the bed to go to the bathroom; I was too scared.

On Sunday it was time for me to go back home, and on the ride back to our house he told me not to say anything to anyone. He said that this was our secret. He also told me that no one would believe me if I said anything, and they would think I was making up stuff. Then he threatened that he would kill my mother if I mentioned it to anyone. I was so scared that I told him I would not say anything, and I kept my word. I did not want him killing us.

Every weekend that I went back, he would show me a little more and touch me a little more. Some nights I was so afraid to get up that I would wet the bed, instead of going to the bathroom. I thought if I stayed in the bed he couldn't get me, so I did. This did not sit well with my godmother, and she let me know that in many different ways. Not only did she fuss at me constantly, she told the kids at the recreation center that I wet the bed. This was very humiliating! If I got up to go to the bathroom, my godfather would mess with me; if I stayed and wet the bed, my godmother would be mad at me. This was all so scary for a little girl. It was a no win situation.

This went on for years. I remember one time when they came to pick me up, I cried and told my mom that I did not want to go with them. She asked me why, but I could not tell her because I didn't want him to kill her. My godmother convinced me that we would have fun and she would buy me food and candy. Why would she say this and then be mean to me?

On that particular night he grabbed me after I came out of the bathroom. I tried to be quiet, but there was a furnace in the floor that made noise when you stepped on it. He took me into the den and sat me on his lap. He caressed my hair and began to grind on my butt; of course, I didn't know what that was at the time. He started to make a strange sound real low, asking me if I liked it, and if it felt good. I kept whining and asking if I could go to bed. He began to move his hips from side to side; I didn't know what was happening, but all of a sudden I felt this warm stuff all over my bottom, and then silence. I guessed it was over; he took some napkins from that end table and wiped off my butt. He smelled my panties and rubbed them all over his chest before he put them back on me. He lit a cigarette and told me go back to bed. I flew back to bed, wondering what had just happened.

On another occasion, I was outside playing by myself when a little girl from across the street came to play with me. I was so excited to have someone to play with. We were having so much fun in the yard and then she asked if she could go inside. I told her no, she didn't want to go in there, but she started to go in the door anyway. I remember dragging her by the arm so hard, trying to pull her back outside because I was scared for her; I didn't want the same thing that was happening to me to happen to her. She went home crying because she thought I was being mean to her; she never came back over to play with me again. This made me very sad because I was only trying to protect her, in the only way I knew how as a little girl.

I was not only scared at my godparents' house, I was also afraid at night at my house, because when I was sleeping I didn't know the difference between my house and theirs. The fear was gripping me so bad that I always wanted to sleep with the lights on, and my sister, who I shared a room with, would fuss about wanting the lights off. Eventually my mom got me a lamp so that I could have a little light in the room. I had nightmares almost every night of him grabbing me. I was terrified of getting out of the bed, so this made me wet the bed at home also, which led to me getting a whipping from my mom. I was more afraid of telling her why I didn't get out of bed than the beatings, so I took the whipping. That fear had a hold on me!

Part IV

The more I went over to their house, the bolder he got. One day his wife had gone to a Church service and left me at home with him and Big Momma. I remember walking down the hallway around noon, and he called me into the den. I thought I was safe because it was daytime; certainly he wouldn't do anything during the day. I was wrong; he was looking at those magazines again, and smoking a cigarette. In the magazine the lady had big breasts, and he forced me to look at them, even when I tried to close my eyes. I had just turned eight and I was so happy and excited about celebrating my birthday. He told me I was a lady now; I told him I was still a child. He told me my breasts were forming, which meant that I was a lady, but my breasts weren't really forming, I was just getting chubby because I was keeping this gigantic secret inside. I asked him if he meant my boobs and he said yes, they would be like this lady in the book. He forced me to look at them; they were big, pink and ugly to me. He told me that mine would look like that someday. I shouted, NO! I don't want that! He said, why not, they're sexy. I asked him what sexy meant, and he told me it meant that you were beautiful and pretty. I wanted to be beautiful and pretty because his wife always told me I was ugly, and so did the kids at school; so I liked the idea of being sexy, if it meant I was pretty.

He told me again that he loved me, and asked me if I knew that. I hated to hear those words because I knew what came next. This time he unzipped his pants and showed me his private parts. I had never seen that before. He placed it in my hand and made me rub it; as I did this, it got harder and harder, and it began to move like it had a life of its own! I was petrified. All of a sudden stuff began to come out of it and he was making those sounds again, very low so Big Momma wouldn't hear him. There in my hand was this warm, sticky stuff. I said, "Yuck, what is this?" He told me it was love; this is what people do when they love each other. I asked if I could go and wash my hands; he told me to be quiet and he wiped my hands with some of the napkins from the end table. He zipped up his pants and told me again that this was our secret. When I left, I ran straight to the bathroom and washed my hands with soap and cried as I did it. I couldn't get that image out of my mind. It was horrible, and I never wanted to see it again!

When his wife came back home, she had this girl with her. She looked a little older than me. I will never forget her! I remember being so excited to have someone a little older than me there; I thought maybe she could protect me and he wouldn't be able to bother me anymore. We played board games together and she would do crossword puzzles while I colored. I'm not sure if he did to her what he did to me, because we never discussed that, but I always wondered.

That summer I went to camp with this same girl on Jekyll Island. There, I met some other girls that were closer to my age. I became friends with a girl named Sandra. I liked playing with her, and I was happy to have a friend. One day I saw Sandra having fun with another girl and I became jealous; I thought she was rejecting me and did not want to be friends with me anymore. I wanted her to be my friend and my friend only, and now she was playing with someone else. This was my first time having a friend and in my mind I didn't know that someone could have more than one. I was very possessive. I was so mad at her, I wanted vengeance, and one day I saw how I would get it.

She was sitting on the edge of the dock facing the deep end of the lake (there was a shallow end for those who could not swim, and a deep end for those who could). I knew Sandra could not swim, so why was she facing the deep end? When I saw her stand up, I thought this was my opportunity to get back at her. I ran as fast as I could and pushed her into the deep end of the lake.

The lifeguard was yelling at me to stop running, while all of the kids including me were laughing at Sandra as she splashed around and struggled to stay up in the water. I knew she could not swim; why would I do something like that to a friend? She could have drowned. She didn't because the lifeguard saved her, but she could have. She didn't speak to me anymore after that incident. I really missed her and regretted doing what I did. I realize now why I did that: hurting people hurt people. It was such a sad reality for me; misery loves company.

Little did I know that I would have my very first encounter with Jesus this same summer. I was around nine years old when I gave my life to the Lord at this summer camp. It was so amazing, I couldn't stop crying and I felt like something different had happened to me. I was sorry for what I did to Sandra the day before; I tried to apologize but she wouldn't talk to me. I knew I deserved this.

We had a revival around the campfire where we made s'mores and hotdogs. We sang songs and played games. One of the games was if you learned John 3:16 you could win this big beautiful white bible trimmed in gold. It was almost as big as I was, but I learned that scripture and won that bible! I was so excited; I would say it almost every day.

When I got home from camp, I ran into the house to tell my mom about my bible. I noticed that our address was 316-A Wilson Apartments, just like John 3:16; I thought that was awesome. My mom found a nice spot for my bible where no one could touch it and where it wouldn't get dirty.

I didn't go back to my godparents' house for a while because I was able to stay at home by myself, and I was happy about that. They still saw me at the recreation center, but there were a lot of people around.

My mom started working at the mill at night and because I was the oldest of my mother's children that lived at home (I had three older brothers that lived with their dad), I had to take care of my younger siblings while my mom worked. She was a single parent so we were alone from around 11pm to 7:30am. Our next door neighbor looked out for us and my mom checked in on us, but because I was the oldest I had most of the responsibility, which made me mature quickly. This was hard sometimes because I had to clean and make sure everyone ate while my mom slept before her shift. I remember looking out the window at my friends playing kickball and wanting to go outside so bad and join them, but we had to be in the house by 7pm. I was responsible for making sure that everything was in order while my mother slept. If my sister or brothers got into any trouble I was punished for it, because I was supposed to look out for them. This put a lot of strain on my relationship with my siblings; I loved them because they were my brothers and sister, but I hated that I was blamed for everything that they did wrong.

Two years later, when I was about twelve, my friend and I, the girl I mentioned earlier, went to spend the weekend with my godparents. I felt safe because she was there with me, but then she got a call that someone in her family had passed away and she had to leave. I went into Big Momma's room and stayed close to her the entire day, because I did not want to give him a chance to grab me again.

Big Momma asked me to go to the kitchen to get her some water out of the refrigerator, where they kept this big pitcher of water. In order to get to the kitchen, I had to pass the den, and he was in there sitting on the couch. When he saw me, I tried to run back real fast, but he grabbed my arms and took me in there again.

This time he laid me down on the couch, pulled down my shorts and underwear and he began to rub his private parts against mine. I was breathing so hard, I almost passed out. He told me that he was going to put it in there; he told me not to worry, that it wouldn't hurt. Tears mixed with sweat were running down my face, and then we heard this very loud cry: CYNTHIA!! CYNTHIA!! WHERE ARE YOU, CYNTHIA?? It was Big Momma calling me; he was so scared, he let me go, pulled up his pants and pulled me back up. I pulled my clothes up and ran into Big Momma's room so fast and went straight into her arms. I was still sweating and my heart was still racing. I remember her holding me so tight as if she knew something had happened. She asked me if I was ok, but I didn't respond; all I did was breath real hard into her chest.

Later on in life when I began to have a relationship with God, The Holy Spirit revealed to me that God used Big Momma to call me at that time so that he would not penetrate me. I cried when The Lord showed me that! He was looking out for me way back then! What an awesome God we serve! I have to take a praise break!

This is sadistic:

One out of every three girls and one out of every five boys are sexually abused in our country. We need to pray for our country!

"Guilt and Shame"

Part I

The summer before Junior High, my siblings and I hung out at the recreation center; they gave us free sack lunches and there were always a lot of activities going on. My godmother still worked there and my godfather had started working for a tractor trailer company that transported cars, but for some reason, he was always around.

One day my godfather told me that I needed to learn how to drive. He said he would be happy to teach me. He brought the front cab of his tractor trailer to the recreation center and he told me that if I learned how to drive in that, driving a car or any other vehicle would be easy for me.

I felt like I could do this; I'd just take some friends with me like I always did. He had to help me get up into the cab because it was so high; I hated that because he had to hold me around the waist. I tried to get my friends to stay with me, but they wanted to go back in and play volleyball or ping pong. They didn't want to sit around and watch me learn how to drive; this was too boring for them. I really wanted their security, but they didn't know that.

He began teaching me in the parking lot; he showed me how to drive forward, reverse and parallel-park using a stick shift. While teaching me he would run his hands up and down my legs, so instead of wearing shorts I began to wear long pants in the hot summer. That way I could not feel his hands on my skin; but since I really wanted to learn how to drive, I tolerated this. Once he felt comfortable with his lessons, he allowed me to drive around the neighborhood, which I was way too young to be doing, especially in a tractor trailer. I would go down side streets that did not have a lot of traffic to avoid the police.

Now that I had this knowledge and could drive at thirteen, I wanted to drive something, but I didn't have a car that I could use. So whenever my older brother came to visit, he would take a nap; while he slept, I stole his car. He had a job close by and he always stopped by to take a nap. It was easy to take his car because you didn't need a key to crank it. I went joy riding all the time and liked the freedom it gave me.

Then one day I took my mother's car while she was asleep. I made sure to bring the car back before she had to go to work, and tried to park it in the exact same place. When she went to get in the car, she noticed right away that it was parked in another location and that the hood was still warm. I was scared because she knew it was me. I thought she would kill me, but our neighbor talked her out of it; she told her that I was just being a teen and that she needed to give me a second chance. I'm not sure if it was the neighbor's pep talk or the fact that she had to get to work, but she didn't beat me that day. I was thankful and learned my lesson; I never touched her car again.

Part II

Everything that happened to me as a child affected my whole life. I started junior high as an overweight, angry teen. I got into fights with both girls and boys; it didn't matter to me who they were. I didn't always start the fights, but I had no problem finishing them. The girls did not like me and my sister because we both had long hair, so they threatened to cut off my sister's hair. My sister was not confrontational, so I fought for both of us. I didn't care. I was so angry at life that I didn't think much of myself; fighting helped me to take out my frustration on others.

I had a wall up; I didn't allow myself to get close to anyone and I didn't let anyone into my life. I was carrying all this extra weight in the natural and in my heart. I had this dark nasty secret and I couldn't tell anyone about it. I recall an older man at the park where I would go walking, asking me why I never smiled; he told me I was too beautiful not to smile. Nobody had ever told me this before, so I didn't believe him. I thought, this guy is just trying to come on to me, I know I'm not beautiful. I didn't want to hear anything like that, and I didn't have time to smile or for him.

Being an overweight teen was hard to deal with. I had so many mixed emotions; I wondered how I really looked to others. Was I worth anything? I felt like damaged goods. I didn't have a boyfriend; why would anyone want to be with me? I knew I did not want anyone to find out about what happened to me. I knew they would wonder why I allowed it, and I knew they wouldn't like me or understand what I was going through! I went to great lengths to hide my secret. I didn't want to get close to anyone because I wanted to make sure no one found out.

The feelings of guilt and shame took over my life. It was like a pillow smothering me.

I always asked myself, why did this happen to me? Why did he choose me? Did I do something wrong? Was it my fault? I was not sure, so I decided I could not trust anyone. My only friend was food; I could trust and depend on food. It was my comfort; it didn't judge me, it didn't use me, and it didn't blame me for anything or misuse me. Yes, food was my medication; it helped me cope with the pain. I became addicted to food like someone who was addicted to drugs. I craved it; I ate in the middle of the night when no one was looking. It made me feel good when I was down, except when I was finished I went back to feeling bad about myself. I was very depressed.

I convinced myself that I was an outcast, the black sheep of the family. I never felt like I fit in anywhere. I looked in the mirror and looked at my family and we didn't even look the same. I was so sad and angry that I began to act out by disrespecting my mother and fighting with my siblings.

I couldn't get along with anyone except my grandmother and my Aunt Alice. I guess because they listened to me and treated me like a baby; they accepted me for who I was. They made me feel loved, and I really needed that. They were my closest relatives and I loved spending time with them. My mom showed me love in her own way, but I didn't recognize it at the time because I blamed her for what happened to me. I realize now that she didn't know anything about it, but I did not know that then.

I often fantasized of being a part of a Caucasian family, because back in the 70's on the television all of their families seemed rich and happy, and our families seemed poor and struggling. Of course, this was only on TV, not in reality, but I didn't know that at the time.

Part III

The food began to take a toll on me and I started gaining a lot of weight. I loved food and did not mind the weight at first, because I knew no one would find me attractive if I was fat. That still was not the case, because one of my junior high school teachers flirted with me and told me I had big, pretty legs. He constantly stared at them when I came into his class with a dress or skirt on, so I started wearing pants all the time.

There were some bonuses to his interest; he would buy me lunch from off campus and bring it back to me and let me eat in his classroom. I guess he figured out that my weakness was food. He also gave me good grades; he asked me what grade I thought I deserved, and of course I said an "A". Would you say anything different?

I was happy for these grades because I had a learning disability, where I struggled with reading and writing. I took extra reading classes to try and get my reading level up to where I needed it to be. I found out later this was called dyslexia. I absolutely hated reading out loud in front of the class. I was terrified of book reports and having to read them in class, so I made things up instead of reading. My classmates had no idea that it was made up, because we all read different books, and my teachers told me I had a great imagination. This approach helped me to get through Junior High.

I had my first crush in eighth grade. I liked this guy but he always picked on me because I was heavy. I thought he was so cute, and my heart melted when I saw him. I was still afraid of boys, so I did not tell anyone, because I didn't have a lot of girlfriends; I only told my sister Tracey about him. Most of the other girls in my class were really small, so I felt like I could not relate to them; I weighed about 125 pounds and was a lot heavier than the other girls.

One day the cute guy was at the Parks and Recreation Center, and some of us girls were looking at him while he was talking with some guys. One of the girls mentioned that he was cute; I was trying to play cool and said, "He's okay."

She must have known that I liked him because she went over and told him that I liked him just to see what he would say. I wanted to hurt her for doing that. I remember this as if it were yesterday; when she told him, he looked over at me and in front of all the other teens he said out loud, "You mean that fat girl? I would never like her." Those words hurt me to my core; I pushed the girl out of the way and stomped out of the door. I walked home alone in the rain and cried the whole way. That was one of the most hurtful feelings of my life; I was wondering why she would do that to me. Why did she have to go over there and say that to him? This is why I didn't like girls; they always betrayed me. I felt like I could no longer trust girls.

This was the first time that my weight had really bothered me, and I decided to do something about it. That summer after eighth grade I worked hard at losing weight; I did jumping jacks, push-ups and ate like a bird. I didn't know much about diets or healthy eating, so I ate bananas, eggs, saltine crackers and ice pops. The ice pops would keep me full when I got hungry. I was determined to go into high school looking good and thin. I lost about 35 pounds that summer and I felt better about myself. I began to gain some self-confidence.

I went to Gaylord's to do some back to school shopping with my mom and siblings, and I was excited about buying my first pair of jeans. I had never worn jeans before because of my weight. I wanted to buy a pair of Calvin Klein jeans. This was the hot new fashion back then, and when I tried them on, they fit perfectly; I loved them, and I looked really good in them. I was excited to show my mom and ask her if I could have them, but she said they were too expensive and she would have to buy it for Tracey if she bought it for me. I began to cry because I really liked the way the jeans looked on me. While crying, I began to think, "How can I get these jeans?" I had an idea; I asked the attendant in the layaway department at the store if I could use the phone (we didn't have cell phones back then) and I proceeded to call my godfather. I had no problem doing this because my mom was around. I cried and told him how much I wanted a pair of jeans for school and my mom wouldn't buy them for me. He came over to Gaylord's right away and brought me the money. I was able to purchase the jeans and an Izod shirt. I was going into high school smaller and more fashionable.

When I went back to school, the same guy that I had a crush on that embarrassed me in front of everyone didn't even recognize me. When he found out it was me he started showing interest, but I ignored him. I thought to myself if he didn't like me when I was fat, I wouldn't like him while I was thin. This is when I first saw Steve in the hallways; he was cute, but quiet and kept to himself. He was very smart and didn't say much. I sat by him in English class and asked him to help me with understanding some of the work, so we became friends. I could tell that he liked me, but both of us were shy in that area.

Remember the guy that I had the crush on earlier, and the girl that told him that I liked him? I found out later she ended up with him and got pregnant by him when we were in 10th grade. I felt like she used me as an excuse to go and talk to him. He was no longer interested in her and started looking at me and all the other girls in our class.

All the guys started noticing me; they used to call me Sugar Hill, like the Sugar Hill Gang. They said I was a brick house. I really liked all the attention, but didn't like it when older men showed interest, which was also happening. I was still very confused, and my whole outlook on love was still twisted because of the things my godfather had told me.

It was hard not having a real father figure in my life; maybe I wouldn't have been so confused about how I should feel about love and how I should act around men. My father lived right over the bridge in Phenix City, but we barely saw him; he was missing from my life. I always wondered if life would have been different if he had been around. I wondered why he didn't want to be around us; was it our fault? I would feel sad when I saw other children with their father. I had an empty feeling and always yearned for what they had. I guess I had to learn to live with what life had given me.

God always causes us to triumph!

"Scars are not a badge of shame, but a sign of Victory!"

"Functioning in Dysfunction"

Part I

Even though I lost all of that weight, when I looked in the mirror I only saw pain and hopelessness. I didn't think I would ever be good enough in the sight of people; this haunted me for most of my young life. I found myself always trying to measure up to what I thought people wanted me to be like. I thought if I acted perfect, they would like me, to the point of sometimes trying to buy love. I would save my money and buy gifts for my mother, thinking that she would love me more. I was the only child that would save money and buy her birthday gifts or cards, trying to get her attention. I needed and longed for her approval, but I felt like she favored my other siblings over me. When she rejected me, I would talk back to her whenever she tried to chastise me. Later I found out that she did this because I was the oldest child at home, and she depended on me to help her.

I also tried to buy friends and tried to fit in at school. I put lots of candy in my purse to give to the other girls, hoping they would like me. I would buy them ice cream and other treats, just so they would be my friends. I got money by selling Avon and sometimes from my godfather. I would give them some of the Avon gifts to see if that would win them over, but it didn't work; they would take my treats but I still didn't have any close friends.

I remember one girl would act like she was my friend on the weekends so that I could buy her stuff, but when we went to school she acted like she didn't know me. One day when we were walking down the hallway to our locker, her friends persuaded her to pick on me and she pushed me and kicked me in the back of my leg. I was trying to ignore her because I was determined to get to the 12th grade and didn't want to get in a fight. I had gotten into so many fights and had been suspended so many times, I kept walking. Then she kicked me again, and this time my knee buckled. I got so mad I turned around, dropped all my books and beat the snot out of her. All of her friends left her there and all the guys that saw it started calling me Mohamed Ali.

The Principal took both of us to his office and I thought I was in big trouble, but Coach Creek saw the whole thing and came to my defense and told the principal that I did not start the fight; he said he saw me trying to walk away. She got suspended and for the first time, I didn't. After this all of her friends were trying to be friendly with me, but I was not interested anymore because I realized they were all phonies; they had left her alone to get beaten up.

That summer before I entered 12th grade, I got into trouble while working for this program called CYO (they helped teens to find summer jobs). The prior summer I worked at Fort Benning in an office setting, filing papers. This particular summer I worked in the Wilson apartments cleaning yards. We were supposed to clean yards and then leave a note in the door that they needed to pay the office for our service.

We were cleaning one lady's yard and she didn't like it; she told us that she did not need our service, and we needed to leave. We kept cleaning because that's what they instructed us to do. She came out into the yard and pushed me and the other girl that was with me to the ground. I immediately went into defense mode; I picked up the shovel and began beating her with it. I remember thinking no one else is going to hurt me, not if I can hurt them first. This was my new way of thinking at this point in my life. All of a sudden I felt someone from behind trying to pull me off of her; it was the lady from next door. If she didn't come when she did I would have hurt her more than just the slight concussion and bruises that she received.

Someone called the police and I asked the girl that was working with me to call my mom. The police came and they had me in the back seat of their car with the door open when my mom arrived. My mom almost went to jail for me that day; she told them to get their hands off of me and to let me out of that car. When she found out that the lady had pushed me, she was ready to beat her again. After we all calmed down, the police told me to stay out of trouble and told me I had to go to court.

I went to court and they put me on a six-month probation. They told me if I stayed out of trouble, the charges would eventually fall off of my record. I lost my job working for the summer youth program, and they didn't allow me to work for the program again. This made me sad because I was planning on using that money to buy things for my graduation.

I had to see a probation officer once a month for six months. The probation officer told me that I had a big mouth and that it would someday get me into a world of trouble. (I believe the enemy was trying to prophecy this over my life, because he knew God would use my mouth for good.) After this incident I found myself trying to think of ways to kill myself that wouldn't hurt! The pain at times was too much. My life was going in a downward spiral.

I reconnected with Steve that summer before the 12th grade while taking senior pictures. This led to us dating for a short time. He was such a gentleman to me; I really liked him a lot. To my surprise, I found out from one of his friends that he was seeing someone else at the same time he was talking to me. When I found that out I was disappointed and dropped him like a hot potato. This was ok, because I was changing schools to attend the same high school that my mother attended; I was also trying to change my environment. We stopped dating, but remained friends for years.

Part II

I began going to Carver High School, where no one knew me; I was trying to make a change in my life. This school was not in my district, so I had to use someone else's address to go there. A girl that I met during the summer was also changing schools, so we decided to ride the city bus together. We tested it out during the summer to make sure we knew how to get there. We had to be at the bus stop at 6:30am to drive across town, just to get to school.

Someone introduced us to marijuana and we started smoking together. We would get off the city bus about two blocks from school, and get high on the way to school, then we would spray Secret all over us so that no one would smell us when we got to school. Going home, we would get high while waiting at the bus stop, and when we got on the bus we would be high as kites; we made fun of all the passengers on the bus. The bus driver flirted with me, which was good because I didn't always have money to pay the bus fare.

One day I got so high it scared me. We were coming home from a dance near Victory Drive when I started feeling really bad; all I could think about was going home. When I finally got home, I filled up the mop bucket with water and poured it all over my head. I was trying to get down from that high and I thought this would help. My aunt had just straightened my hair and I messed it all up. I remember telling God if he could get me down from this high, I would never touch that stuff again. When I came out of it, I kept my promise and never smoked another joint again. My friend thought I was crazy when she asked me to get high with her and I told her I was never doing that again. I also told her it only made you feel good for a little while, but when you came down all of your troubles were still there. I know now that God was with me, even way back then.

Part III

During my 12th grade year I met this guy at the YMCA that made me feel like I was the only girl in the world. He lived off of Brown Avenue and he would ride his bike uptown to Hamilton Road, where we lived at the time. We talked on the phone until after 12am most nights, because my mom worked nights. We dated my entire 12th grade year and he promised when we graduated in the fall we would get married. Finally, someone wanted me and loved me, or so I thought!

He purchased a ring from this jewelry store downtown called Change and Things. He gave me the ring on Valentine's Day; I was so happy! Since I was wearing his ring, he started pressuring me to sleep with him, but I couldn't. I found it hard to even kiss him for the first time; my past was still haunting me.

For several months he kept pressuring me and telling me that he loved me. I hated those words because that's what my godfather would tell me before he abused me. I had mixed emotions because I really like him, but did not want to sleep with him. Then he said it, "If you love me, you would have sex with me." So we were supposed to be married in June, and in April I slept with him. It was awful! It was painful! I cringed the whole time! He made those weird sounds like my godfather used to make. I didn't like it at all and I thought it would never end. I felt that warm stuff on me and it grossed me out; I wanted him to leave right away, but he seemed to like it and wanted to stay. He kept hugging me and telling me how much he loved me. All I wanted to do was take a bath. I felt dirty, and all I could think about was my godfather and that last experience that I had with him. I just wanted it to be over.

He called me every day after that and came over to my house on the weekends, but I didn't sleep with him anymore. I told him we would wait until after we were married. I wanted to do the right thing. A month later we were getting ready for our graduation and prom. He was supposed to go to the prom with me, but he backed out two days before the prom. I'm not sure why he did that, so I called one of my other guy friends and he was nice enough to take me. I had to borrow my sister-in-law Maryjo's blue prom dress. She had several dresses for me to choose from, but the blue one was beautiful. We didn't stay at the prom very long, because he wanted to take me to dinner at Red Lobster. He was a perfect gentleman; he gave me a corsage and paid for everything, including our pictures. We had a good time together, but I only saw him as a friend.

It was time for graduation and I needed money for my cap and gown, yearbook and senior trip. I struggled to figure out where I would get the money for the cap and gown, senior pictures and all the other graduation expenses, since I could no longer work for the CYO. Then it came to me: I'll call my godfather and make him pay for everything; he owed me that much. I nervously dialed the number and hoped my godmother would not answer the phone. I was relieved when he answered the phone. I asked how he was doing and he informed me that his wife had passed away. Instead of feeling sad, I had a smirk on my face when he told me about her death.

I started crying and telling him that I was graduating and didn't have enough to pay for all the expenses. He asked me how much I needed, and told me to come over to get it. I took three of my girlfriends with me; we sat and talked to him for a few minutes and then I told him we had to take the car back. I was not staying there any longer than I had to.

A couple of weeks later, we had our senior trip to Six Flags over in Georgia. I felt so sick the whole time I was there. I got on the roller coaster and when I got off, I threw up. I thought it was because I had eaten a lot of junk food that day, but even after the trip I woke up feeling sick every day. I couldn't stand the smell of bacon cooking. I told my friend that I rode the bus with how I was feeling, and she asked if I was pregnant. I told her no way! She asked if I had slept with my boyfriend, and I told her only once, that we had decided to wait until after we were married. She told me it only took one time to get pregnant. I didn't realize that you could get pregnant after the first time. I was petrified! I knew my mom would kill me.

My friend talked me into going to this clinic off of Wynton Road; she assured me that they would not tell my parents, and it was free. All I had to do was watch a video about abortion. I agreed, and we went to the clinic together. They gave me a cup to pee in and came back in a few minutes and told me I was pregnant. I was shocked, I was scared, and I was crying; this was awful. I thought, "What am I going to do now?" The nurse told me I had a few options; I could have an abortion, have the baby and give it up for adoption, or keep it.

I was not in any position to make that kind of decision, so I told her I would go home and tell my mom and see what she said. I was so scared to tell my mom. I envisioned her being very mad and yelling at me. She was mad and started cursing and fussing, but didn't act as bad as I thought, because my sister had gotten pregnant before me, so the blow to me was not that bad. She let me make the decision and told me if I chose to keep the baby, I had to take care of it because she wouldn't.

I didn't know anything about having a baby. I had met some girls at the clinic and they told me different resources that were available to me if I decided to keep the baby, for example, the Right from the Start program and the Wic program.

Part IV

I remember being so glad to have made it to my 12th year in school, and now this; something else to deal with. When I told my boyfriend about the pregnancy, he changed. He stopped calling and stopped coming over. This was crazy; I was wearing his ring and I didn't know what was going to happen to me and my baby or where I stood with him. Then I started hearing rumors that he was dating someone else, a girl that was a virgin. I was so disappointed because I was a virgin before he begged me to sleep with him and promised me that we were getting married. I guess that's why he didn't want to go to the prom with me. I felt so stupid; how could I fall for that?

I was six weeks pregnant when I graduated, so Tanisha walked across the stage with me. Three weeks after we graduated from high school, he came by to see me. I asked him what was going on with him, and he told me he was not ready to be a father. Well, that was tough, because I was pregnant and it was not going anywhere. He tried to convince me to have an abortion, but that was not an option that I was willing to consider. I told him I would raise the baby by myself if I had to; he did not object and he left.

I cried for most of my pregnancy, because I could not believe that he left me after he swore that he loved me and would marry me. I got through some tough months where I couldn't afford maternity clothes and I didn't have anyone to talk to. The few friends that I had turned on me; it was a lonely time in my life.

I pawned the ring that he gave me and used the money at a thrift store to buy some maternity clothes, and one of the girls that lived down the street from me gave me some of her clothes.

I thought things couldn't get any worse, but guess who showed up at my door a few days after my birthday? My ex-boyfriend. I was eight months pregnant, and I was shocked to see him, I thought he had a change of heart and was coming to see how I was doing. But to my surprise, he proceeded to tell me that he had married another girl on my birthday, the same girl that he was dating after we slept together. I was wondering why he would come by to tell me this, but then I realized he wanted to sleep with me again. He told me it was ok to sleep with him because I couldn't get pregnant, since I was already pregnant. I threw him out of my mom's house. I was so upset that I wanted to kill myself, but I didn't want it to hurt and I didn't want to harm my baby, so I just cried almost every day.

One night I felt this awful pain around 1:30 in the morning, and when I got up out of the bed to go to the bathroom, my water broke. I knew it was time! I got my mother's husband to take me to the hospital. I was afraid because I had never been to a hospital before. I checked myself in and called my Auntie and my grandma; they told me they would come by the next morning, because they did not drive at night. Being in labor was the worst pain I had ever felt, especially going through it alone. My mom came by to check on me before she went to work and my Auntie, grandma and uncle came the next morning; my grandma and uncle stayed with me until I had the baby. All of the pain was worth it when I had my beautiful daughter on December 16, 1983 at 2:15 in the afternoon.

When I first saw Tanisha, it was the happiest I had been in my life, but I was also scared for her. She was so beautiful and small and innocent; would someone do to her what they did to me? No, I would have to kill them! I was going to protect my baby at all costs! Her dad came to the hospital to see if she looked like him. One of the first things he asked me was, "Will they make me pay child support if he didn't sign the birth certificate?" I threw a pitcher of water at him, then called the nurse and had him put out of the room.

When I got home from the hospital, our house was crowded; my sister and I still shared a room, she had a baby and I had a baby, so four of us shared the same room. Raising a baby in my mother's house was not easy, so I began to save the little money that I made with the intention of getting out of there. When the opportunity arose, I moved into a small apartment down the street. It wasn't the nicest place, but I had some place to call my own. I purchased my furniture from the thrift store and paid $30 dollars for a refrigerator that had a hook for a handle. I could not afford the gas bill, so I had to boil water to take a bath and to bathe my daughter.

The apartment was next to a Church that I visited when I got depressed, but they rejected me because I wore short skirts and looked different from them. They made me feel uncomfortable and looked down their noses at me, so eventually I stopped going.

Part V

Life was hard in my 20's; I had to move from my little apartment to the projects. I could no longer afford the apartment, and in the projects the rent was based on your income; they also included water and gas in the rent. This was good for me because I didn't have gas at my last place, so now I could take hot showers.

My next door neighbor, Sheila, became my friend. We were both single parents with daughters, so we could relate to each other's situation. I was working two jobs to make ends meet, one at Taco Bell and the other as shift leader at Del Taco. Sheila worked at night and went to school during the daytime.

The worst part about being a single parent was leaving my daughter, and finding someone trustworthy to watch her. Sheila and I took turns watching each other's daughters. I trusted her because we were a lot alike.

Eventually I had to put Tanisha in preschool because Sheila was starting her clinicals. I saved some money to buy her some clothes for school. I decided to shop at Sears because they had cute, reasonable clothes. When I got to the register, the cashier asked me if I wanted to open up a Sears card to pay for my purchases. I felt like I had nothing to lose, so I completed the application and to my surprise, I was accepted.

I was so excited to have my first credit card. I paid for Tanisha's clothes with the card and was able to buy gas and groceries with the money that I intended to use to buy her clothes. I remember being so excited that I had a credit card. Sears always sent one of those big catalogs for free when you were a card holder. When I got my catalog I couldn't wait to look through it to see if I could afford to buy anything. When I got to the lingerie section and saw all of those women in their panties and bras, I began freaking out and having flashbacks of the magazines that my godfather used to make me look at. I threw that catalog on the floor and never looked at it again. Eventually I threw it in the trash.

I chose not to be in a relationship for a while because between my godfather and Tanisha's dad, I was turned off from the whole idea of love and men. They were affecting my mind, my attitude toward men, and my entire existence. I wanted to trust, but it was always in the back of my mind that someone was out to get me.

Steve and I rekindled our friendship, and we began talking again, but only as friends. I shared with him my concerns about not having enough to pay rent, daycare, my car note, car insurance and food (I was not receiving any government assistance because I was making too much money). He suggested we make an arrangement, that he would give me money to help with the bills and I would sleep with him, no strings attached. Even this was hard for me at first.

One time after sleeping with him I felt so dirty and unclean, even though we used protection. I went to take a shower, trying to wash away what had just happened. I cried out to the Lord, "Please help me, please help me," but I thought he didn't hear me because of how I was living (now I know that he did, because the bible says while we were yet sinners, Christ died for us and he loves us), but in my mind I felt like I was a prostitute even though I was only sleeping with one guy. I knew that this was wrong.

This worked out for a while, but then my feelings started to change towards him. I began to really like him and I wanted more than the arrangement that we had. He was naturally a sweet person, but I didn't know how to tell him that I was beginning to like him and I certainly did not want to get hurt again. So one day, I asked him what would happen if we began to fall in love with each other. His answer was that we would cross that bridge when we got to it, so I took that to mean he was not feeling the same thing that I was feeling, so I stopped seeing him. I cut all ties and I didn't answer his calls; I was upset because I let him have my heart and he didn't take care of it.

I was so hurt, I found myself using men to get what I wanted. I started dressing in ways to get attention; I dressed provocatively and seductively. I wasn't sleeping with anyone anymore; I would string them along and take their money and make promises that I knew I was not going to keep. When the time came to sleep with them I would make up excuses why I couldn't make it. This was a dangerous game, but in some way I felt like I was getting back at my godfather and the other men in my life that had hurt me.

One weekend I went to a barbecue with my brother Eric. His girlfriend had a cousin there who was interested in me; we talked the whole time and before leaving, he asked me for my phone number and I gave it to him. He called me that night to see if I made it home safely, and we started dating. He was different from all the other men that I used; he had a good heart and was very kind to me.

This man really cared for me and my daughter, but I couldn't bring myself to love anymore; it hurt too much. We dated for six months, but I was not ready to sleep with anyone else. One night my daughter was not at home, she was over at Sheila's house, and I slept with him. About a month later I started feeling sick and couldn't stand the scent of the chili sauce at work. I had to constantly go in the bathroom at work to throw-up. I remembered the last time I felt like that, I was pregnant with Tanisha; so I went back to that free clinic and found out that I was pregnant again.

I beat myself up because I could not believe that I had done it again. I did not want to be a single parent with children who had different dads; so when my boyfriend asked me to marry him, I said yes. I did not want to have another child out of wedlock, so I married him for security.

After we got married, he moved me out of the projects. This was a big day for me. I had only dreamed of being out of the projects and my dream was finally coming true. I also only had to work one job, since I had someone to help me with the bills.

One of my family members needed help with her daughter and my husband was kind enough to allow her to stay with us. She was good company for Tanisha; they were like sisters.

Being married did not change the way I felt about men, and even though my husband was a good man, I never let my daughter or her cousin sit on his lap; I didn't even want him to kiss them on the cheek. I was still paranoid. I wondered about everything he did and was constantly watching him when he was around them.

I began to relax a little as time went on and tried not to focus so much on the bad things that could happen, but to focus on the positives; the fact that he loved me, my daughter and her cousin and treated them like they were his own children. Just being married while pregnant was so very different from my first experience. This time I could afford maternity clothes; my husband bought me flowers and anything I wanted to eat. I also had a baby shower, so that I had some things for the baby before he was born.

When I went into labor, my husband was there with me; I didn't have to be by myself this time. I was in labor for twelve hours, but at least I had his support. Because of the length of my labor, the baby's heart rate began to go down. I was scared when the doctor told me they had to perform an emergency C-section. This was my first time being put to sleep or having any major surgery. We prayed together and asked God to help us through this; we didn't know much about prayer or God, but we gave it our best shot.

They put me to sleep and when I woke up I had a 9lb 10oz baby boy. I was so excited to have another baby; I had someone else that would love me unconditionally and this made me happy. I was also happy that he was a boy; I felt like I didn't have to be so worried about a boy. My husband decided to name him Dominique, after Dominique Wilkins, the basketball player (I found out later that Dominique means belonging to God).

Four years later, I got pregnant again, and around this time my husband got promoted as a car salesman. He started hanging out with all of these women from work who smoked and drank with him. I didn't drink or smoke, so I felt left out and began to have a lot of mistrust in my heart, which led to us having constant arguments and physical fights. He would go to the bar with some of his co-workers that were women and this made me jealous. The stress of his new job made him smoke and drink even more; this put a lot of pressure on our marriage.

I believe all of the stress of constantly worrying and arguing with my husband led to me having a miscarriage at five months into my pregnancy. I was distraught; I blamed him for everything. I really wanted another baby, someone that I could pour my heart into and know that they wouldn't hurt me. I became very depressed. I knew I still had my other two children and their cousin to take care of, but I couldn't pull myself together.

My husband and I decided to start going to the same Church that rejected me when I was single. This was the only Church I knew and they had a new Pastor that I liked. This made things a little better between us, because we were trying to live a better life. We both got baptized. We didn't know what this meant, but we were trying to improve our lives.

I left Del Taco and went to Mrs. Winners. The owner of Mrs. Winners liked me because I always went above and beyond what they asked me to do. Within seven months, I became a shift manager. I got pregnant again while working at Mrs. Winners. When I was seven months pregnant I slipped on the greasy floor at work and fell, and I had to go out on workman's compensation. When I had my baby boy, TaShawn, I spoiled him rotten because of the miscarriage before him. I was so happy to have another baby to fuss over.

Life was good for a while, and then we began to have some financial problems. The transmission in our car went out, so we only had the car that belonged to the dealership. This presented some problems because I used to sell newspapers and had to be at the building at five in the morning to pick up my stack of papers. I also had to take Tanisha and Dominique to school, and my husband had to be at work at 7:30am. I was not able to use the dealership car to do any of this. My husband and I didn't know what to do, so again I turned to my godfather to ask for help.

I still felt like my godfather owed me, and I needed to make him pay. I told him about our one car situation and he gave me one of his cars that needed some work done to it. He would come over to our house to help my husband fix the car, and we visited him when we needed money. I always kept my children close to me when he was around. I never let them hug him. I didn't tell my husband what happened to me when I was a child because I thought he might not love me anymore and leave me. I went along as if nothing had happened.

This caused even more stress in our marriage, because my husband smoked and the smell of cigarette smoke reminded me of my godfather. Having my godfather around and constantly smelling the smoke on my husband made it difficult for me to be intimate with him. When those moments came around, I would draw back and imagine myself on a beach in Hawaii or some other place, anywhere but there; that was my only way to cope. I wanted to leave him, because this was not fair to him; he deserved more, he deserved someone that would love and appreciate him. I felt like a phony, but I also wanted that security of being married.

Enlighten the eyes of your understanding!

"Your identity is not based on your past, but on the clarity of your future."

"Living in Deceit"

Part I

We were married for nine years and he constantly accused me of cheating on him, so we fought all the time; not just with words, but also physically. I assumed he was cheating, since he kept accusing me and because I already had trust issues.

We were getting ready to get our house painted and have wallpaper put up. I had several guys come out to give me an estimate. I ended up giving the job to one of my ex-school mates who remembered me and gave me a good price. He was very attractive, tall and charming, and had great hair. He was half white, half black; this was definitely the type of guy that I was attracted to.

He wall papered the kitchen and painted the living room and came by on Valentine's Day to take care of some loose ends in the kitchen. I was all dressed up in a tight fitting red dress with a split down the front. I was waiting for my husband to come home to take me out to dinner, to celebrate Valentine's Day. I had gotten someone to babysit the kids, so when the painter came by, I was home alone. When he walked in the door he began complimenting me on how beautiful I looked in that red dress; he knew how to charm a lady. He pointed out that if he were married to me, he would not keep me waiting. He told me how much he liked me in school but he was too shy to say anything. I was really enjoying all the compliments and attention. But he was also making me nervous.

It was getting late and my husband had not come home yet, and it was time for the painter to leave. I walked him to the door and to my surprise, he turned around and kissed me on the mouth, and I kissed him back. I couldn't believe what I had done. I was thinking, "Why would I risk my marriage of nine years and do something silly like that?" I told him he had to leave; he walked away and all I could do was stand behind the closed door and argue with myself for being so stupid. I realized I was really attracted to him (of course, the devil will not send you something you don't like).

When my husband finally came home around 8:30pm, he came in with some flowers, but I didn't want any flowers. I was really upset with him for having me wait so long. I felt like I paid a babysitter in vain. He told me he was trying to make some money and sell a car, and the paperwork took longer than he expected. It didn't matter to me what he was doing, it was Valentine's Day and I was really pissed at him; I had gotten all dressed up for nothing. I felt like he had put his work and his friends at work before me. We went and picked up the children and, after getting them ready for bed, I got in the bed and turned my back to him. I pretended as if I was asleep, but I was really thinking about that kiss.

The next day the painter called several times to apologize for what he did, asking every time if I was ok. I told him it was ok, I was married and I should not have done that. He asked me if I still wanted him to come by to do the bathrooms, and he said that since he stepped out of line he would not charge me for the kitchen. But I was not having anyone give me anything for free. I told him he could come by and paint the bathrooms, but I would still pay him for the kitchen.

He came by the next Monday to paint the bathrooms. All the kids had gone to school, except for TaShawn; he was not old enough for school yet. I showed him into the bathroom and made myself busy in the kitchen getting breakfast ready for my son. After a while the painter called me to take a look at the color, asking me if I liked it. Then, right there in my master bathroom, he kissed me again, and I kissed him back again! What was I doing? I ran back to the kitchen to make sure TaShawn was still in there and did not see what had just happened.

He continued his charm even after his work was done. On several occasions he bought me jewelry. He would put all kinds of gifts in the mailbox; then he would call me on the phone and tell me to go and look in the mailbox. He was reeling me in and I didn't even realize it.

On several occasions he put cash in an envelope in the mailbox and he even left his credit card in the mailbox, to help me buy clothes for my children. He called every day, several times a day, to see if I needed anything. He was charming and seductive! He knew exactly what to say and do.

One day he convinced me to meet him at a hotel in Phenix City while all the kids were at school and my husband was at work. I didn't know anything about Phenix City, so we met on Broadway and I followed him to the hotel. After three kids, and nine years of marriage, this was my first time enjoying being intimate with a man. The secrecy intrigued me at first, but then it started to wear on me.

Our relationship lasted for eight months, and then I could not take the lies and deceit any longer. My conscience would not allow me to go on. I had to break it off with him; even though my body longed to be with him I wanted my children to have some kind of stability with their father, because I never had that with mine. I was determined not to be another statistic, so I decided to make my marriage work. This was not easy for me because he kept calling me, calling my friend that I used to go walking with and calling my brother. My friend and my brother were the only two that knew about our relationship. He told them that he loved me and he wanted to marry me. It finally died down after he realized I was serious about not seeing him again.

Part II

The affair was over, but the repercussions of it were not over for my husband. He kept asking me if I had something going on with the painter, but I could honestly say no because I didn't anymore. Then when he asked me if I had ever slept with him, I crossed my finger behind my back and told him no (I thought if I crossed my finger, I could lie and it wouldn't be a lie). He knew I was lying because he said I always looked him in the eye when I was telling the truth, but looked away when I was lying. But I would never admit it; I was prepared to take it to the grave. I wanted the security of being married and wanted my children to have their father.

Our marriage was rocky because of all the lies and deceit. I don't think he trusted me anymore, he started acting differently towards me and I became distant because he kept questioning me about the painter. I didn't want to deal with it anymore; it was over for me why wouldn't he let it go. We were just going through the motions, after that I wanted to leave him but I wanted my children to have a stable home so I continued to stay. He bought me a GMC Truck trying to improve our relationship. I was happy about the truck, but kept thinking "If I left him who would make the payments." I loved him but I was not in love with him.

Part III

A few months later I found out that Steve's wife had died; this was my old friend from high school, the guy who I had the arrangement with at my apartment. I was sad and reached out to him to comfort him. When I heard his voice on the phone, he sounded really depressed.

I asked my husband if I could go over to check on him. When I got over there he had started drinking and looked really depressed. I tried my best to comfort him; I told him he could call me if he needed to talk.

He began calling me and I confided in him about my marriage and how it felt like it was over. We started seeing each other on a regular basis; we met at the mall or at Lake Bottom, and sometimes at his apartment. He had two kids, Jasmine and Terrance. Sometimes I would take my three children over there to play with them.

Those old feelings started to resurface; he was hurting and I was hurting too. One thing led to another, and we were back to our old selves. Steve knew that I wasn't happy in my marriage, so he encouraged me to leave and come and live with him. He said he would pay for the divorce and take care of all my expenses. I did not want to hurt my husband, so I had mixed feelings about Steve's offer.

One day when the children and I came home from Steve's apartment, I had really decided again that I would stick it out with my husband, when he met me at the car door. He was mad and asked where I had been. I told him I was out visiting a friend. He kept asking me what friend, and then he told me he had followed me and saw that I was at Steve's apartment. I asked him why he was following me and he told me I was his wife, so he could follow me if he wanted to. I knew this was not good, so I started to get back in the car when he grabbed the necklaces that the painter had bought for me; one of them broke and cut my neck and his hand. I told the children to stay in the car and locked the door, and we drove back up to Steve's apartment. He followed us, but Steve would not let him in.

The children and I spent the night with Steve and the next day I went home when I thought my husband was at work, but he was there waiting for me. He told me he only wanted to talk, but he was pulling me and being very rough with me in front of the children. I knew that it was over; in my mind, I knew that I was done. I told him that I was filing for a divorce and we went back to Steve's place. When I got there, Steve got down on one knee and gave me a big diamond ring and asked me to marry him. He promised that he would take care of me and not hit me or mistreat me. I said yes because I still had those old feelings for him, so it didn't take much to convince me. We began the difficult process of my moving out.

I had planned to move out that Friday, but when I went back that Thursday night to get some clothes for me and the children, my husband had been drinking and told me to take all my stuff and leave. I called Steve, my cousin and my brother and we moved everything out of the house and into Steve's apartment.

Steve had purchased a house, but it was not move in ready yet so we had to rent a storage room to store everything. For the next few months everything was a whirlwind. Immediately I filed for a divorce; as soon as the divorce became final in May, Steve and I got married in July.

We had a small wedding over at the Community Center and the Pastor from the Church that my ex-husband and I were attending married us. I repeated the vows that were given to me, but when we got on the dance floor to do the first dance, I made it clear to Steve that I wasn't obeying anybody, so if he thought I was going to obey him we could annul this marriage right now (these were the thoughts of an insecure person).

We couldn't go on a honeymoon because we had five kids and had just purchased a home. I wasn't working, only selling Home Interior, so Steve was the sole provider. He had two children and I had three; we were the black Brady Bunch. The children got along very well because they were already friends and had been playing together. They did not quite understand what was going on, because one of them kept asking if their dad was coming to live with us too. I felt like God was redeeming me for the baby that I had lost; he gave me double and I didn't have to go through the pain of childbirth.

Honesty is the best policy!

"Being transparent will expose the enemy!"

"Stuck for Too Long"

Part I

God had a setup for me. I was switching channels on my television one morning when I ran across this woman minister telling her story about how her father had molested her for years. Of course this grabbed my attention. I watched her and saw the power and authority that was coming out of her; she was funny and seemed happy. I wondered how she could be so happy after having a past like that. I didn't think it was possible at that time in my life. What she said stuck with me and I could not forget her. I started watching her every day.

One day my ex-husband called me and I was watching the news about a tragic accident. I had an upset feeling in the pit of my stomach, that this accident had something to do with me. He told me to get some clothes on and come down to the police department as soon as possible. I asked him what was going on, but he wouldn't tell me; he said to just come as soon as you can, that my niece (the one that used to live with us when we were married), was in trouble. He told me not to bring the children with me, to get someone to watch them.

As Steve and I drove to take the children to my mother-in-law's house, I began to see an open vision (I had been having visions on and off for years, but I didn't know what they were); my niece's life began to play before my eyes. I saw her as a baby and then as a child growing up in my house and then as a teenager. Then the reel of the film stopped and started flapping. It was like those old movie reels, and the reel ran out. When I saw it stop, I immediately knew what it meant, I knew she was gone. I started crying, "No, God, no." Steve kept asking me what was going on, but I couldn't tell him what I saw.

When I got out of the car to drop the children off, I began to throw up. Steve told me to pull myself together because I didn't even know what had happened yet, but I knew she was gone; God had already revealed it to me.

When we got to the police station my mom and my ex-husband were there crying, and I knew before I saw her why they were crying. I had to go back with her mother and identify the body. I passed out and her mother passed out. Seeing her like that was just awful; I asked God to remove those pictures from our minds, and he did.

I had just spoken to her two hours before; this changed my life forever. After her death, I wanted to die. I thought of all the things that I could have done differently. If I had changed anything, would she still be alive? There was nothing I could have done that would have changed this outcome. This affected both me and my children; we all had nightmares for a while. I tortured myself over what I could have done. I lost so much weight agonizing over her death. I was in a rut and didn't know how to get out.

I remember going out on my back deck and crying out to God for help. I told Him I needed Him in my life, I didn't know what else to do and I wanted what the lady on TV had.

That weekend my brother and his wife came to visit us and invited us to the Church they were attending. The name of the Church was New Life; how appropriate, as I needed a new life. I knew that I needed to go, but I began making all kinds of excuses why I couldn't go; I didn't have any church clothes, I needed to get my hair done (I was used to the fashion show churches). My brother convinced me that this Church was not like that; he said it didn't matter what you had on, you could come as you are.

Steve and I finally agreed to go. On Sunday morning we got up, got our children dressed and went to New Life Church on University Avenue. When we got there everyone was so nice and friendly; the guy in the parking lot opened our door and welcomed us to the Church. The music was great, and I could feel the love in that place. I became afraid when some people started speaking in another language, and I didn't understand what was going on. This was all so new to me. I had never experienced this type of service before.

The preaching was good; Pastor Vince made everything so plain that even my children could understand him. When they made the altar call, to my surprise, Steve jumped up and went to the altar. I didn't know what to do, so I took our five children and followed him. I had experienced God when I was nine, but I certainly did not have any type of relationship with Him. Steve gave his life to the Lord, I rededicated my life and we became members of the Church. I still felt like I was stuck in the past, and I was not going to allow anyone to tell me what to do; I was not ready to submit to anything or anybody. I wasn't going to allow anybody else to misuse their authority in my life.

Part II

New Life was a different experience for me, and we got involved right away; Steve joined the Ushers, I joined the choir and both of us worked in the Children's Ministry. Even with all of this, I still did not understand what having a relationship with God was about. I thought I had to follow all the rules and regulations and do good to get rewarded, and if I did bad things I would be punished. I had never been a member of a Church before, because the other church that I attended with my ex-husband made me feel rejected. I was trying to be perfect so that I could fit in; remember, I always thought I was not good enough.

I was hard on my children; I did not allow them to listen to any music other than gospel and I did not allow them to watch too many TV shows. I never let them spend the night at anyone's house for fear that what happened to me could happen to them. I never let them go to birthday parties alone or to a slumber party if there was a father figure in the house. This was my way of protecting them, because I felt like I was not protected as a child. I didn't know at that time that God could protect them; I thought it was my job to keep them safe.

I know now it was a warrior spirit that God put on the inside of me, not to war in the natural, but to war in prayer for my children and also for all the children that were in my sphere of influence. This was one of my reasons for working in the Children's Ministry, so that I could pray for the children. If I saw a man with a little girl around the age that I was when I was molested I would automatically begin to pray for the girl, because my mind always went back to what happened to me.

One day my family and I were in McDonald's, and a man was in there with his daughter; she was around the same age I was when I was molested, and she was sitting on his lap and then he kissed her on the mouth. I cringed and started freaking out, then I began praying for her. I'm sure he did this innocently, just showing affection for his daughter, but that was a trigger point for me; my mindset was not changed yet, and the weight of my past was still on me. Steve was wondering what was wrong with me and he asked why I had to always respond like that. He was compassionate and wanted me to share what was going on with me, but I refused, because I had all these walls up and I didn't want to let him into that dark place. I wasn't sure if I even wanted to be in that place myself. I had not told him what had happened to me yet, so he could not understand why I always reacted like that. I told him you never know what's going on; everyone needs prayer.

I was still too afraid to let him know what happened to me. I wanted him to understand, but I wouldn't let him in. It was tormenting me because every time I saw a dad with his child alone, all those feelings would try to overtake me; I wanted to be free, but I still didn't know how.

This way of thinking led to me being strict with myself, my children and my husband; I was paranoid about everything that concerned my children. I didn't want their lives to be messed up like mine, so I tried to overdo everything. I thought I needed to control their music environment, their television environment, and their friend environment. I thought if I kept all of this away from them they would have a better chance at life, and would not have to grow up so fast like I did. I felt like after doing so many things wrong in front of them (the divorce and cheating), I wanted them to see something right; I wanted them to have a better example.

I didn't realize that life happens, and I was not helping them. I should have let them make some decisions within a controlled environment so that when they were away from me, they would not be so easily influenced and make bad decisions.

I thought anything that was not gospel music was worldly and I wouldn't even let my husband listen to jazz music. One day I came home and threw away over two hundred CD's. I filled up two trash cans, and my mom thought I was going crazy and told me to give the CD's to her, but I thought I would be partaking in her sin if I gave them to her (someone had shared this scripture with me and I was following it). I went out and scratched them up so that she would not take them out of the trash.

Steve was the same way; he began throwing all his alcoholic beverages down the drain in the kitchen. I knew when the trash men came they must have wondered what was going on with us; we had trash cans filled with CD's and liquor bottles.

I went from one extreme to another. I was saved, but I was still bound and stuck with trying to be perfect. I was trying to measure up to people instead of God. I had to learn it's not what you do for God, but what Christ has already done for us. I knew God was in me, but I felt like there was more to him than what I knew. I was determined to find out what it was.

I began to listen to everything on TBN; I woke up to TBN, went to sleep with TBN and listened to TBN while cleaning. I read my bible for 35 to 40 minutes a day and prayed for another hour, and kept a journal. I would get mad and beat myself up if I didn't do this every day. This might have been overkill, but it made me stronger in my relationship with God.

I was so determined to know more about God, when they made the altar call one Wednesday night I went up to be filled with the Holy Spirit. It didn't happen like I thought it would, I didn't get filled immediately, and Kaycee Lewis, one of the Ministers at New Life, told me that it was in me but I was trying too hard to figure it out. She told me to relax and not to think about it; she said I could be in my car praising him and it could happen. But I was thinking in my mind, "How can this happen if someone is not there to pray with me?" I was overthinking it and trying to rationalize how it would happen instead of looking to Jesus. (The Bible says to look to Jesus, the author and finisher of our faith – Hebrews 12:2.)

To my surprise, the next day I was worshipping God in my car on my way back from dropping the children off at school, I just starting praising God with a song that was playing and just like Kaycee said, I began speaking in an unknown tongue. It was just rushing out of me. I was speaking and then in my mind I was saying, "Oh my God, oh my God, I'm doing it." I could not believe it was actually happening! I was so excited I couldn't wait to tell my husband, but I could not reach him on the telephone.

I was waiting for him when he got home. Filled with excitement, I told him what had happened to me that morning, but he didn't believe me; he told me to do it again. I said, "I don't know if I could just do it." He could not understand, and I was not sure if I could do it again. I didn't quite understand what was going on myself.

The Holy Spirit began to help me to hear from God more and not to be so rigid and paranoid about everything. It helped me with my children; I began to pray about things instead of not letting them do anything. When they came and asked if they could go anywhere, I sought peace through the Holy Spirit; if I felt peace about what they were doing then I would allow them to go, and if I didn't feel peace, then I made them stay home. This was the new order of my house: allowing the Holy Spirit to lead and guide me.

God revealed himself to me as my Father and I began writing letters to him and signing them "Your daughter Cynthia". I loved my prayer time, and it was just awesome to be in his presence; I had never felt this much love from a father before. I needed this because I didn't have a father figure in my life, so I loved the fact that I now had one, and he was the greatest of all Fathers!

Part III

Learning how to submit to authority was one of the hardest parts of this journey of letting go. Starting with my husband, I had promised myself that I would not submit to anyone ever again. I likened submission to someone scrubbing me with a brillo pad; it hurt, and didn't feel good to my flesh.

I would often call Pastor Marcia for help. She gave me scriptures to stand on and she would pray with me and impart so much wisdom into my life. The more I submitted, the harder it seemed. I would be in the shower talking to God and he would reveal to me that I needed to apologize to my husband for any disagreement that we had, whether it was my fault or not. I would ask God why I had to be the one who had to always apologize, but God was teaching me how to be humble and to trust him (remember I didn't trust anyone, so I had to start with trusting God).

After I learned submission, it became a benefit for me. My husband started to change his attitude towards me because I was changing my attitude towards him. He treated me even better than he was treating me before. He began buying me gifts, leaving me love notes and sending me love texts. I appreciated this more than he knew.

Trusting God was like a roller coaster ride; I had held on to my pain and distrust for so long, that when I began releasing everything to him I felt like I was free falling without a parachute. I was not in control anymore, and I didn't know how to handle giving everything to God. So one day I just showed up at Pastor Marcia's house crying; she and another lady that was there at the time surrounded me in prayer, and we all began worshipping on her living room floor. It was so beautiful; I felt God's comfort and his peace, I felt like I could trust him, that even though I didn't know what he was doing, I could trust him. Pastor Marcia gave me some scriptures to meditate on. One scripture that stands out was Proverbs 3:5-6: "Trust in the Lord with all your heart and lean not unto your own understanding, in all of your ways acknowledge him and he would direct your path." Time flew by; I got there around 10 in the morning, and when I looked up it was time to get my children from school.

I finally had someone who was nurturing me; I never had this in my life besides my Grandma and Aunt. My Grandma had passed away and my Aunt had Alzheimer's, so Pastor Marcia was filling that void. She was a great influence in my life, and she helped me to become the mom and wife that I am today. She taught me how to pray over my marriage and my children. She told me to allow Steve to lead; this was hard for me, but slowly I began to let go and let him rise up to his position as leader of our household.

I remember one day, Pastor Marcia told Jasmine and TaShawn that they could have a sleepover with Maria. When the time came for the sleepover, I came up with about 50 excuses why they couldn't stay. She didn't know why I was coming up with those excuses; it's not that I thought anything would happen to them, but I was still struggling with trusting others and I had never let my children spend the night anywhere before. Pastor Maria was not having it; she was a woman of integrity, and she said she had promised them, so she was keeping her word.

This was a major breakthrough in my life, because I began to allow my children to spend the night at some of my other Church friends' houses. That was the beginning of my journey to trust that God would protect them. I knew it was still my responsibility to watch over them, but not to the point that I was too paranoid about allowing them to go anywhere or do anything.

Cast your cares on Jesus!

"Past pains can be a heavy burden, but Jesus' love can lighten the load!"

"Choosing to Change"

Part I

I would love to say that when I made the choice to change, it was easy, but it wasn't; it was a process. I had to make a conscious effort to change and work at it daily. Romans 12:2 says, "And be not conformed to this world: but be ye transformed by the renewing of your mind, that ye may prove what is that good and acceptable will of God." God wants us to be renewed in the spirit of our mind, because this is where all of the battles take place.

Another change that I had to make was learning to receive. This was very hard for me. I always thought everyone had an evil motive; if they did anything for me, I thought they wanted something in return. For this reason, I did not want anyone doing anything for me. This was my attitude before I met Christ. This was one of the hardest lessons for me to learn, that someone could give me a gift and not expect anything in return.

I had to trust God to know that he would bring the right people in my life to love me unconditionally, and to give without expecting anything in return. He has done that for me over and over again. I have friends that I can call on and they will do anything for me, and I will do the same for them. I know that they actually love me for me, not for what I can do for them.

Because of my learning disability, I never liked to read, but God began to show me some books that I could read to help renew my mind. Not only did I read them, I enjoyed reading them and some of them I read twice. I read a book by Joyce Myers called, "Battlefield of the Mind"; this book helped me to speak over my thoughts, instead of being quiet and hoping bad thoughts would go away.

Another book called "Hung by the Tongue" by Francis P. Martin, which taught me to watch the things that I allowed to come out of my mouth. There is a saying, *"Sticks and stones may break my bones but words will never hurt me!"* This is a lie straight from the pit of hell! Words hurt, words have destroyed some people. They form your thinking. Whatever words are spoken can be the difference between a stronghold of failure being formed, or one of success. This is why the Bible says that "life and death are in the power of the tongue." Let's choose to speak LIFE!

John Osteen wrote a book called, "There Is a Miracle in Your Mouth." This helped me to make declarations over the things that I want to see in my life and the lives of my family members. These books, along with the Bible, began to help me transform my thinking.

I knew that God had a plan for my life, but I was not sure what that plan was. I knew that I wanted more and I was determined to get it. I woke up early in the mornings while everyone was still asleep to talk to God and study the bible.

I knew I was changing; I was so hungry for more of God that every time there was a service at Church, I was there. I longed for him and his presence. During this time, Pastor Vince was doing a series on "Who are you yielding to?" He said whoever you are yielding to, that's who you will obey. I decided right then and there that I was yielding to God at any cost. Even the dark places in my life, what happened to me in my childhood, my marriage, my finances, my children, my relationships with all my family members, I yielded it all to God. I really loved God; I just didn't realize how much he loved me.

I feel like God began mending all of my relationships, but I still struggled with forgiving my godfather. I didn't realize that not forgiving him was hurting me more than it was hurting him. This struggle kept showing up in my weight; I was constantly battling with my weight like a seesaw. I would lose weight, then gain it back again, because what was on the inside was still affecting my outside.

I prayed every day that God would show me how to forgive him. Then Pastor

Vince invited me and Steve along with some other leaders at the Church to go to a conference in Chicago with Dr. Bill Winston. Pastor Winston spoke about calling those things that be not as though they were; he said not to speak what you see, but to speak what you want to see. This stuck with me; I decided to start speaking what I wanted to see.

When we got back home from the conference, every morning when I woke up I would say, "I forgive him, I release him." As soon as I decided that I was going to forgive my godfather, Satan began attacking me in my dreams and in reality. One day I was in a department store shopping with my granddaughter, and when I looked up from my shopping cart, who should I see but my godfather. My granddaughter was around the age that I was when I was molested and I don't know what triggered it, but when I saw him I panicked. He was walking with a cane and I wanted to knock him out and take that cane from him. I left all of my things in the shopping cart, grabbed my granddaughter and ran out of that store. I got into my car and held my granddaughter real tight and rocked her back and forth in the seat, asking God to please help me. I thought I was over this. I called my friend, Ms. Mary, to pray with me. I thought I had forgiven him, but all of those old feelings started rushing back again.

I began having dreams about him all over again. I remember waking up one night in a cold sweat; I was screaming and shaking, because in my dream I was running from him.

Steve asked, "What's wrong, what's going on?" I asked him if he could just hold me. I had not told him what had happened to me yet because I was so afraid that he would blame me and not love me anymore.

By now I knew that my godfather would not kill me or my mom, but I was still ashamed of what had happened and thought Steve would think it was my fault. I felt that maybe I had done something wrong, that maybe I should have done something to stop him or maybe I should have told my mother what was going on. I also felt guilty about continuing to take money from him as a form of punishment towards him. Satan had me holding on to this because he knew that it would keep me bound.

I felt like a rape victim that was afraid to tell her story because maybe she was dressed provocatively or was drinking, or maybe out late. She knew they would make her feel like it was her fault and that she was the guilty party; instead of the accuser being blamed, they would blame the victim. All of this was keeping me from telling anyone about my past.

Finally, one night after having another bad dream, Steve asked me to please tell him what was going on. I finally released everything to him. I did not hold anything back. I had shared a few things with Ms. Mary, but this was my first time telling it all. This was such a load off of me; it felt like a burden was lifted. For the first time in my life I had told someone everything that had happened to me. WOW! I wish I had done this sooner.

His reaction was totally unexpected; instead of looking at me with an accusing eye, he held me and stroked my hair and let me know that it was going to be ok. He told me that God would take care of me and so would he. It was amazing to me, because I had held out all of this time thinking it would be awful, and he was more understanding than I ever imagined. He began being protective of me, which was different for me because I had always looked out for myself.

He didn't hate me or leave me like I thought he would. He loved me even more and was more compassionate. Before, when I acted out when I saw a little girl with an older man he didn't understand, but now he knew that he needed to comfort me. This was the beginning of the rest of my life!

Part II

God began to line things up for me. I met a lady named Gaynell at New Life, who introduced me to conferences. She began taking me to women's conferences in Atlanta, Georgia, at Pastor Dollar's Church. This was so amazing because I had never seen a mega Church like this before, except on TV. Even the bathrooms were beautiful. Then we branched off into prayer conferences. Every year we went somewhere different. God was exposing me to different people and different places.

Sometimes I didn't have any money to go to the conferences, but God would work amazing miracles for me to get to them. One day, after singing "Let the Praise Begin" at New Life Church, someone came up to me and gave me the exact amount for the airline ticket to a prayer conference in Branson, MO with Kenneth and Gloria Copeland. I knew this was God, because I had not told anyone how much it would cost to go to that conference.

When we left for the conference, I only had $10 to spend. Gaynell had taken care of the hotel room, so I felt guilty asking her to buy food, too. I didn't mention to anyone what I had. The hotel served breakfast and one of the other ladies that went with us had shared her snacks with me, so I kept those in my purse in case I got hungry. The first night of the conference, I went to the bookstore and asked if they could change my $10 into ones; my thought was, I could put $2 in the offering every night and still have $4 to buy something to eat. I remember going into the bathroom at the conference, crying out to God and asking Him why he had me here with all these women who had money when all I had was $10. I had to borrow a cell phone to call back home, my purse was all torn up, I felt very uncomfortable and out of place, but I was hungry for the word and I wanted to learn more about prayer.

While at the conference, I met a lady named Charlene. She was sitting in the row behind us and just kept looking at me. Finally, she came over to me and introduced herself. She began prophesying over me and told me that I was a prayer warrior and a worshipper. I wasn't sure how to act when this stranger started speaking to me. She said that God had told her to give someone this harp broach that she had made; she said He told her she would know who to give it to. When she saw me, she knew that the broach was for me. I was still skeptical, but I took the broach. She then took my hand again and put some money in it. When I got to the car and looked, it was $40. I thought to myself, "Thank you, God, for favoring me."

We went out to eat that night and I was happy to be able to order a salad and know with confidence that I could pay for it. When we got the check, Gaynell's sister paid for my salad, so I still had my $40.

The next night when we went to the conference, Charlene greeted me and told me that she had special seats up front for me and my friends. When we got up to the second row, there was a sign that said 'reserved for New Life Church.' I thought, "God, you are so amazing!" How befitting that the sign said New Life Church and we were from a Church called New Life, and God had given me New Life! As we took our seats, another lady named Marsha that had prayed a powerful prayer the night before began to prophesy over me, saying that I was a prayer warrior and a worshipper; the same things that Charlene had told me the night before. I thought to myself, "Is this really happening?" I told God he had to confirm what these ladies had prophesied over me.

After the service, they were selling a prayer series for $90. I thought, "Lord I would really like to have that, but I don't have that kind of money." Then Billye Brim got up and said, if you don't have the money and want the series, you can go back to the table and tell them that you don't have the money and they will give it to you for free. Isn't God good?

So I'm standing in line for my free series and a tall gentleman behind me from Russia begins to prophesy the same things that Charlene and Marsha had said. I knew God was real, but he just kept revealing himself to me constantly. What an awesome experience that was, to meet such wonderful people and experience God's favor on my life. I came home from that conference with more money than I left home with.

Another conference that I attended was the Columbus Faith Conference at New Life Church. Dr. Bill Winston was preaching that night, and he said we needed to sow our way out of our lack. Well, I had a lot of lack, but I didn't have anything to sow, or so I thought. A couple from our Church had gotten married earlier in the month and they had given the wedding guests a Sacagawea coin (worth $1). This coin was all I had. The members of the Church began going up and throwing money on the altar. I thought, I don't have anything to sow, and God reminded me of the coin that I had from the wedding. I began reasoning with God that I was not going up there to give a coin when everyone was giving so much. I was embarrassed, but I had to be obedient so I went up at the end of the service and gave the coin to Pastor Winston and told him it was all I had. He hugged me and he said, "Don't downgrade your seed, a seed produces what is needed." I was so excited for the hug!

The next day my father-in-law asked me to take him to the farmer's market. When I got there, he began buying things for himself and told me to pick out what I needed. This was unusual for him; my mother-in-law would give freely, but never him. He bought me all the groceries that I needed and then when we got in the car, he gave me $100. I was amazed that God had given me a hundred fold back on that $1 coin that I had sown. This was my first time experiencing the hundred-fold blessing!

Part III

I was filled with the Holy Ghost in 1998, and God called me into the ministry on January 9th, 1999. I preached my first sermon in 2000 in Maryland, miles away from home. I was invited to speak at a Women's conference and Min. Delia and Sis. Latrilla travelled to Maryland with me. The title of my sermon was "Taking off my past pains." I had the ladies take all the hand bags and purses that were around and strap them all around me. When I went out to preach, I said, "I know you all are looking at me crazy, wondering why I came out here with all these bags on me, but this is how some of you look in the spirit with all your past pains hanging on you." They immediately liked me because I was preaching about something I knew a lot about. The people at the Church treated me like a queen and paid me to preach. I was in shock. The doors of opportunity were opened for me to minister, but I wasn't looking to get paid, I was just excited that I had a chance to go share God's Word in love. On this trip, I got a chance to visit the White House and the Lincoln Memorial.

Then I ministered in Roanoke, Alabama. My car broke down on the way there; the enemy was trying to do everything to stop me from getting there. The Church gave me $75 for preaching and that was exactly how much it cost me to fix the car. I told the car repair man that I had to tithe of this money, and asked him if he could fix it for $65, and he did.

The furthest I ever went to minister was Nassau, Bahamas. This was truly an amazing experience for me and my family; they paid for me, my husband and our five children to go on a cruise. This was our first cruise and our children's first airplane ride. They also paid for our airfare and then paid for me to preach on the cruise. We had our own cabin, the girls had their own cabin and the boys had their own cabin. God allowed my children to experience abundance; they were getting room service and all the food they could eat. They were not used to this because at home, I only had $15 to $20 a week to shop for groceries for seven people, with no government assistance. They were used to lack, so this was their opportunity to see God's abundance in action.

It was so amazing that God allowed me to go to all of these places before I ever preached here in Columbus, Georgia. This was an awesome experience. I was doing something I never thought I would be doing and getting paid to do it. I am thankful to God that he has always given me opportunities to minister his Word. I never went anywhere soliciting to preach; God always opened those doors for me, and he has always shown me favor.

Be renewed in the spirit of your mind!

"Renewing your mind is the key to living a changed life!"

"Letting Go of the Weight of My Pain"

Part I

During the process of writing this book, I took my grandchildren down to the park and there was an older man and his granddaughter there. She was around that age that always caused something to trigger in me. This time was different; I was at peace, I didn't act all emotional like I usually did and I didn't feel the urge to pray for her. I was able to have a casual conversation with him. This was a victory for me!

God never meant for me or you to live our lives in the past! He paid for our new life with His own blood. He had and has a plan for our lives. The enemy tries to keep you bound to your past by fear, condemnation, guilt and shame. But you can be free from the weight of your past pains. This freedom comes by allowing God to come into your life and yielding everything unto him. These weights keep you from moving forward.

John 8:36 says, "Therefore if the Son (Jesus) makes you free, you shall be free indeed."

Hebrews 12:1-2 says, "Lay aside every weight, and the sin which so easily ensnares us, and let us run with endurance the race that is set before us, looking unto Jesus, the Author and finisher of our faith." This same scripture talks about how Jesus endured the cross with joy; can you imagine having joy while hanging on a cross, being spit on, lied about, talked about, betrayed and beaten? But our Lord had joy because He knew that you and I would have the opportunity to receive Him as our Lord and Savior and be redeemed from the snares of the enemy into God's Kingdom.

This is something we must understand, that the devil studies our habits and our lives from the time we are born to see what we respond to. He tries to distract you from the future that God has planned for you. If he can keep you living in the past and keep bitterness and hatred in your heart, he will. He tries to get us to look at our imperfections and flaws; it's all a part of his plans to keep you distracted from Jesus, who is the real focus. Our identity would no longer be in our past pain or our own ability, but in Christ who is the hope of glory (Colossians 1:27).

The enemy always tried to make me feel bad about not having a father figure in my life, but now I know that I have a FATHER! The greatest Father, Jesus Christ! It is the devil who is fatherless! Not knowing this truth in the beginning affected me in a negative way. It made me look for approval from people, especially those I looked up to. I was looking for love in all the wrong people and places.

Colossians 2:10 says, "We are complete in Christ." When I found this out, my life changed. When I believed it and received what the word of God had to say about me, the blinders and weight began to fall off! No longer did I believe the lies that were playing in my head. I knew that God truly loved me, not because I was trying to be good, but that He loved me in spite of me. Jesus really paid for me, and you to have a new life in Him. This relationship is the most powerful relationship that I or you could ever have. Not religion, but relationship; there's a big difference.

God told me, His blessings on my life are not based on how good I am or the goodness of anyone around me; they are based on the finished work of His Son, Jesus! It is because of that finished work that he desires to do good things for me. His desire is to love and bless me. So I'm not at a disadvantage like I thought when I was growing up. I'm at an advantage because I have His favor, love and mercy on my life!

Part II

I want to leave you with some life changing confessions that I have incorporated into my daily routine. Through my daily time with God, my mind has been renewed as I have learned to no longer identify with my past pain and suffering, but to recognize the pain and suffering that Christ endured on our behalf.

My mind was being renewed; I realized that it wasn't about me! We're not called to be perfect, and we don't have to be. The God we serve IS perfect! He has NO spots or blemishes! We have to know that our identity is in Christ Jesus alone! We have to know that we are children of God! We have to know that our righteousness was not of ourselves, but in Christ Jesus! Only what he did at the cross will last! We have to know that he truly wants us to have a new life and a new way of thinking, a life filled with his amazing love for us.

Just as natural parents desire to do well by their children, our heavenly Father desires to do us good. Not just good, but better than good! (Acts 10:38, Matthew 7:11) The enemy cannot trick or fool us any longer into thinking God doesn't love us. We know in our hearts, not just our heads, that we are loved by almighty God and that His love would never fail us.

Remember these words as you take your journey to your truth, that God loves you! His love covers a multitude of sin (1 Peter 4:8), and that his grace is sufficient for us today and every day (2 Corinthians 12:9). I want you to know that God is not out to get us, but to love us. For God so loved the WORLD, not just Christians, but the entire World (John 3:16).

In the Old Testament, look at how God allowed Abraham to plead for Sodom and Gomorrah (Genesis 18:32). Abraham pled with God to spare Sodom and Gomorrah if at least 55 righteous people could be found in the city. As Abraham continued to decrease the number of people required for God to spare the city, he stopped at 10. What if Abraham had continued to decrease the criteria down to 1 person? What do you think God's response would have been? I personally believe that even if asked to spare the city for 1 person, that God would have done it. My relationship and understanding of the nature of God is that He would have spared the city for even 1 righteous person; that is the mercy of our God! This gives you something to think about. If Jesus had been sent to the cross to save just 1 person, He would have still suffered the cross for that 1 person.

Our God is a God of many chances, not just a second chance! I can't explain it, but when you realize that this amazing, awesome God loves you unconditionally, it makes you fall in love with Him over and over again!

Thank you, Jesus; you don't give us what we deserve, but you give us what was already paid for with your blood!!

Confessions:

- I am the righteousness of God in JESUS Christ – 1 Corinthians 1:30, Romans 5:21

- I am God's child – John 1:2, Romans 8:16

- I am redeemed by the blood of the Lamb – Revelations 5:9

- I am favored by Almighty God – Psalm 5:12, Proverbs 14:9

- I am the head and not the tail, above only and never beneath – Deuteronomy 28:13

- No weapon formed against me will prosper - Isaiah54:17

- I am victorious – 1 Corinthians 15:57

- I am complete in Christ – Colossians 2:10

- As He is so am I in this world – 1 John 4:17

- I am a new creation in Christ Jesus, old things are passed away – 2 Corinthians 5:17

- I am forgiven by Almighty God – 1 John 1:19

- I am loved by Almighty God – John 3:16, Romans 5:8

- I am the apple of God's eyes – Psalm 17:8

I give out of the love of God!

I pray out of the love of God!

I love out of the love of God!

I see through the love of God!

Prayer:

- Father in the name of Jesus, I pray for the power to forgive any and all people who have ever misused, abused, hurt or harmed me in any way.

- I pray that your very presence will invade my heart to know the truth about your love for me.

- I pray in the name of Jesus that every dark secret in my heart will be released into your nail pierced hands.

- I pray that I will no longer be a victim but I am victorious through your word. I pray that I will see myself as you see me; happy, strong, free, healed and whole.

- I pray that every strategy of the enemy against me and my identity will be of no effect against me. I now choose to release the weight of my past pains and fears to YOU, in Jesus' mighty and matchless name, Amen.

CPSIA information can be obtained
at www.ICGtesting.com
Printed in the USA
LVOW03s0857231017
553426LV00006B/790/P